MANAGING YOUR
MONEY AND FINANCES™

Getting a Credit Card

Xina M. Uhl and Ann Byers

Rosen
YA™

New York

Published in 2020 by The Rosen Publishing Group, Inc.
29 East 21st Street, New York, NY 10010

Copyright © 2020 by The Rosen Publishing Group, Inc.

First Edition

Library of Congress Cataloging-in-Publication Data

Names: Uhl, Xina M., author. | Byers, Ann, author.
Title: Getting a credit card / Xina M. Uhl and Ann Byers.
Description: First edition. | New York : Rosen Publishing,
2020. | Series: Managing your money and finances | Includes
bibliographical references and index.
Identifiers: LCCN 2018048116| ISBN 9781508188520 (library
bound) | ISBN 9781508188513 (pbk.)
Subjects: LCSH: Credit cards—Juvenile literature. |
Finance, Personal—Juvenile literature.
Classification: LCC HG3755.7 .U45 2020 | DDC 332.7/65—dc23
LC record available at https://lccn.loc.gov/2018048116

Manufactured in the United States of America

CONTENTS

INTRODUCTION **4**

CHAPTER ONE
What Is Credit? **7**

CHAPTER TWO
Fine Print and Its Effect on You **16**

CHAPTER THREE
Taking the Plunge into Credit **23**

CHAPTER FOUR
Dangers of Credit Cards **30**

CHAPTER FIVE
Credit Scores and Why They Matter **39**

CHAPTER SIX
Protecting Your Credit **47**

GLOSSARY **55**
FOR MORE INFORMATION **57**
FOR FURTHER READING **60**
BIBLIOGRAPHY **61**
INDEX **62**

INTRODUCTION

n an ideal world, each of us would pay for everything we want and need with money we have saved in our bank accounts. That may work for small purchases like groceries or fuel for our vehicles, but what about large purchases like cars, homes, and college educations? Most people do not have thousands— or hundreds of thousands—of dollars saved and ready to use. Purchases that have a high-ticket price usually require some sort of a loan, or credit, that the borrower will repay over time.

Credit—and credit cards—have a lot of advantages. Credit makes it possible for people to use things (such as homes) while they are still in the process of paying for them. Having one or more credit cards is a great convenience when it comes to buying things online, renting a car, reserving a hotel room, or making emergency purchases that you cannot afford at the time. The modern world is easier to navigate with credit cards. Yet there is a price to pay for this convenience. Unless you manage your credit

A credit card can make life easier as long as you know how to be its master and not let the balance, interest, and fees add up.

wisely you can find yourself in serious debt. Such debt has very real consequences, affecting job prospects, the ability to rent a home or apartment, and problems when you try to obtain banking services and loans.

Credit cards come with a number of risks. It is important to read all of the terms and conditions of your credit cards because the lender may include penalties and charges that you need to watch out for so that you don't end up paying more than you expect. It is all too easy to think you need to only pay the minimum payment amount on your credit card each month, but such practices mean you will end up paying a lot more than you may expect.

Identity theft is another danger you will face. In this digital world, it is important to keep your private information private. Hackers and thieves are always on the lookout for ways to game the system, and if you are unfortunate enough to become a victim, you may end up losing money and having to repair your credit.

It may seem like getting a credit card is a necessary step to adulthood, and it is true that it provides a lot of convenience. Still Shakespeare's advice that he gave four hundred years ago in his play *Hamlet* still applies: neither a borrower nor a lender be. While it is always a good idea to keep from borrowing on credit as much as possible, by having a good plan and knowledge, you can make use of credit wisely.

CHAPTER ONE

What Is Credit?

C redit is nothing more than money that is borrowed. The moneylender, or creditor, provides you with the funds so that they can earn interest, or a percentage of the amount, on top of the loaned money when you pay them back over a period of time. It's not free money—it comes at a cost. Creditors are businesses, and they cannot stay in business unless they make money.

Two types of businesses lend money: financial institutions and retail stores. Financial institutions lend money for one reason; stores lend money for a different reason.

Credit from Banks

Financial institutions are banks, credit unions, and loan providers. Just like stores, they have a product to sell. Their product is money. Stores buy and sell clothing, books, and other items.

HSBC is a provider of banking and financial services with nearly four thousand offices worldwide.

Financial institutions take in and give out money. They use money to make more money. The main way they make money is by charging interest.

Interest is a fee paid for using money. When you deposit your money in a savings account, the bank pays you interest because it will use your money. When you borrow money from the same bank, you pay the bank interest because you are using the bank's money. Financial institutions pay interest to depositors at a low rate. They charge interest to borrowers at a higher rate. Let's look at an example:

You deposit $1,000 in the bank. The bank pays you 2 percent annual interest. You make $20 at the end of one year, assuming that you do not put in or take out any other money during this time.

$1,000 x .02 = $20

The bank lends the $1,000 you deposited to ten people. Each person borrows $100. The bank charges the borrowers 5 percent interest. Each borrower pays $5 in interest ($100 x .05 = $5). The bank makes $5 per person x 10 people = $50.

The bank made $30 on your $1,000:

Money the bank made in interest	$50
Money the bank paid in interest	-$20
Money the bank made	$30

Thirty dollars may not seem like much, but if you add up thousands of loans for thousands of dollars, banks can make a lot of money. Banks make money because they receive more in interest than they pay out in interest. Banks also make money by charging fees for some of their services.

Just because the bank loans out your money does not mean your money is not there when you need it. Banks are always taking in and lending money. They have plenty of cash reserves. Even

GET A LIMITED-TIME INTEREST RATE WITH A QUALIFYING DEPOSIT
EARN UP TO

1.25% | **0.39%**
Promotional Interest Rate | Annual Percentage Yield with a minimum $25,000 balance

Stop in for a special rate on a Citi Savings Account.

citi.com/savingspromo

citi
Welcome what's next

Interest rates on credit cards vary from one credit card to another. Be sure to compare interest rates carefully before you apply for a credit card.

if a bank fails, a government agency called the Federal Deposit Insurance Corporation, commonly known as the FDIC, protects depositors by insuring their bank accounts. The FDIC pays people the amount in their account up to a certain amount. Right now, that amount is $250,000.

Credit from Stores

Stores also make money by extending credit. A store's credit card lets you borrow money from the store. For example, when you buy a shirt with a store credit card, the store is lending you the money to buy the shirt. It is expecting you to pay the money back when you get your credit card bill. But the store does not charge

Most department stores allow you to purchase items with a store credit card, which can be used only there, or a regular credit card that can by used in many places.

you any interest on that money if you pay it back on time. So, why would the store lend you the money? Because it wants your business. Stores make money by selling their products. They offer credit to get people to come into their stores and buy their goods.

However, if you don't pay your bill when it is due, the credit will begin to cost you. Most stores let you pay off the bill a little at a time, but they charge interest on the amount you still owe. If your payment is late, they charge late fees.

Types of Credit

There are basically two types of credit: secured and unsecured. A secured loan is a safe loan—safe for the lender. The lender is pretty sure it will not lose the money it is loaning because the borrower has something of value to back up, or secure, the loan. For example, say you buy a car for $7,000 and make monthly payments. A financial institution is lending you the $7,000 and is expecting you to pay the money back—with interest. The institution is safe in lending you the money because if you don't pay, the institution can take the car, sell it, and get its money back. The car secures the loan.

Something of value that is used to secure a loan is called collateral. When you purchase a car on credit, the car is the collateral. When people buy a home, the house is the collateral. Other expensive items, such as furniture, appliances, and jewelry, can also be collateral.

Most credit cards are unsecured. That means you have no collateral backing up your promise to pay. If you buy games, electronics, or school supplies with a credit card and do not pay the bill, a store does not repossess the goods. Many, many stores issue credit cards—all of them unsecured.

Expensive purchases, such as a new television, can be purchased with unsecured credit cards, meaning the store will not repossess your goods if you don't pay the bill.

Visa and Mastercard

Banks also issue unsecured credit cards. Unlike a store card, which can be used only in the store or group of stores that issued it, a bank credit card can be used in lots of places. It generally has a Visa or Mastercard symbol on it. Visa and Mastercard are associations of thousands of financial institutions. The banks that belong to Visa can issue credit cards with the Visa logo, and the institutions that belong to Mastercard can issue cards with the Mastercard logo. These cards carry the logos of the bank that issued them and the Visa or Mastercard symbol. They are universal charge cards, meaning they are accepted in many stores, restaurants, and other businesses.

Do Credit Cards Benefit You?

Reasons to Have a Credit Card:
- Carrying a card is safer than carrying cash.
- You can often get your money back if something goes wrong with a sale.
- If you have a serious emergency, you can borrow money right away.
- You can buy items online or over the phone.
- You are building a credit history, which will help you when you are ready for major purchases, such as a house.
- A credit card bill is a good record of your purchases.
- Some cards let you earn bonuses, like money back, air miles, and discounts.

Reasons Not to Have a Credit Card:
- If you don't keep track of your purchases, you could spend more than you realize.
- If you are not careful, you might spend more money than you can afford.
- If you don't pay promptly, you end up owing lots of money in interest and fees.

When you use one of these cards, you are borrowing money from the bank. For example, if you charge a movie ticket on your bank Visa card, the bank pays the theater and you get a bill from the bank. Many people like to use bank cards because they can

An ATM card, also called a debit card, gives you the convenience of not having to carry cash. Debit cards deduct directly from your bank account.

carry just one or two cards and use them at most of the places where they do business.

Other Kinds of Cards

Every card your bank offers is not a credit card. Banks also offer automated teller machine (ATM) cards and debit cards that look very much like credit cards. You use an ATM card at an ATM to do your banking business—deposit money, withdraw cash, make payments, etc. You cannot borrow money or buy anything with an ATM card.

You do buy things with a debit card. Often, a bank issues one card that is both an ATM card and a debit card. Using a debit card is just like writing a check. When you buy shoes, for example, with a debit card, the bank subtracts the money from your account right away. (The word "debit" means "subtract.") The bank sends the money from your account to the shoe store. You don't receive a bill because you paid for your purchase when you swiped your card. You may receive a statement that shows how much you spent, but the money is already gone from your account.

In summary, when you use an ATM or debit card, the bank moves your money immediately. When you use a credit card, you move your money later. A credit card does not give you more money to spend; it just gives you a little more time before you spend it. In fact, it might even make the things you buy cost more! You'll read more about this in chapter 2.

Credit sounds very simple: You borrow money, and then you pay it back. Some creditors charge interest, but others don't charge interest if you pay the money back in a certain amount of time. Credit cards let you borrow, but ATM and debit cards do not.

However, credit is actually a bit more complicated. Many people have serious financial problems because they don't manage credit well. How do they get into so much trouble? How can you avoid credit disasters? What if you lose your credit card? What if someone else tries to use your card? How do you get a credit card in the first place? Knowing the answers to these questions will make you credit smart.

CHAPTER TWO

Fine Print and Its Effect on You

If lenders want to stay in business, they have to make money—money that comes from you in the form of interest and fees. Different creditors have different charges, or terms. You will need to read the fine print (usually in very small letters) in your credit card agreement to find out how much it will cost you to borrow money.

When you open a charge account, you receive a cardholder agreement. The US government requires any bank or business that issues a credit card to give the person receiving the card a written statement that explains the conditions the issuer places on the card. The cardholder agreement has to tell what the interest rate is, what other fees might be charged, how the required payment is calculated, and what cardholders can do if they think their bill is not accurate. This agreement is usually written in tiny letters, so it is called the fine print. Sometimes, it is written in language that is not easy to understand, and many people simply ignore it. But knowing what to look for in the fine print makes you credit smart.

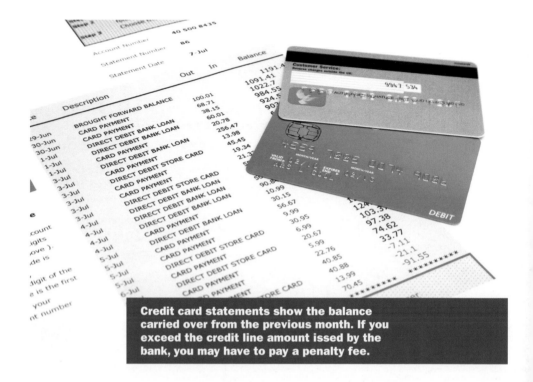

Credit card statements show the balance carried over from the previous month. If you exceed the credit line amount issed by the bank, you may have to pay a penalty fee.

Installment and Revolving Accounts

There are two types of credit accounts: installment accounts and revolving accounts. Car and school loans are installment loans. Some other big-ticket items are often purchased through installment loans, too. With an installment loan, you pay the same amount every month until you have paid the loan back. Sometimes, you can make extra payments so that the loan is paid back sooner than originally agreed. But if you miss a payment, you will be charged a fee.

An installment loan is given for one item. If you buy a refrigerator, you might take out one loan. If you want to buy a dishwasher, you would have to get a new loan, even if you buy it from the same company. Once you pay the loan back, you close the account.

A revolving account lets you make one agreement and borrow over and over again. It is like a revolving door. You purchase what you want up to a certain amount. The lender sends you a statement—a bill. You pay all or part of your bill, and you might charge more items. Then, the process starts again. The lender sends you a new statement once a month. Credit card accounts are revolving accounts.

Many credit card companies do not charge interest if you pay your bill in full when it is due. If you pay back what you borrow every month, using revolving credit does not cost you anything in interest. But if you do not, the lender charges you interest, and interest can add up to large amounts very quickly.

Figuring Out Interest

Lenders calculate interest as a percent of the money you borrow. That percent is called the interest rate. Credit card companies use an annual percentage rate, or APR. The APR is the rate they charge for the whole year. But they charge interest every month. To find out how much they charge each month, divide the APR by 12. So, if the APR is 18 percent, every month you are charged 1.5 percent ($18/12 = 1.5$).

When you get your statement, if you do not pay all you owe by the due date, you are charged

Introducing

5% Back

**at Whole Foods Market®
and Amazon.com**

with the Amazon Prime Rewards Visa Card*

amazon.com/amazonvisa

prime

VISA
Signature

D. BARRETT

Providing you with a rebate based on your purchases is a common tactic for credit card issuers to get you to apply for a card.

one-twelfth of the APR on whatever you owe. If you don't pay the entire bill the second month, you are charged in that month another one-twelfth of the new amount you owe. The interest can really add up. For example, let's say you spent $500 and planned to pay it off at the rate of $25 per month. How much would the loan cost you? Let's figure it out at an APR of 15 percent and a payment of $25 per month.

Month 1	$ 500.00	Total borrowed
	-$ 25.00	Payment
	$ 475.00	Balance owing
	+$ 7.13	Interest charged (475 x .015)
Month 2	$ 482.13	New balance
	-$ 25.00	Payment
	$ 457.13	Balance
	+$ 6.86	Interest
Month 3	$ 463.99	New balance
	-$ 25.00	Payment
	$ 438.99	Balance
	+$ 6.58	Interest
Month 4	$ 445.57	New balance
	-$ 25.00	Payment
	$ 420.57	Balance
	+$ 6.31	Interest
	$ 426.88	New balance

In just four months, you would pay $26.88 in interest. The total interest for the entire loan would be $78.95. That means when you are finished paying the loan, you will have paid back the original $500 that you owed, plus an extra $78.95 in interest. So, the total amount that you would pay for this purchase is $578.95. And it would take you twenty-four months to pay it off.

Credit card companies actually have a number of different ways to calculate interest using the same APR. The above method is the adjusted balance method because it makes the calculation, or adjusts the balance, only once a month. It is the simplest and results in the lowest interest.

But most companies use the average daily balance method. They calculate your balance each day and find out what your average balance is for the month. Then, they charge interest on that figure. This makes the interest that you owe a little higher.

Credit card interest rates are either fixed or variable. A variable rate can go up or down, depending on what is happening in the world of finance. A fixed rate, in theory, does not change. However, lenders can change the interest on their cards as long as

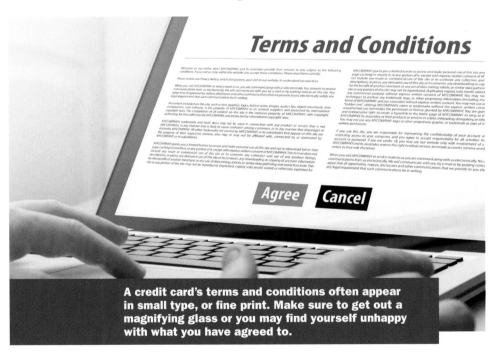

A credit card's terms and conditions often appear in small type, or fine print. Make sure to get out a magnifying glass or you may find yourself unhappy with what you have agreed to.

they give fifteen days' notice in writing. And the writing is often in very fine print.

Understanding the Terms

To make sure that you pay the least interest possible, you need to understand some of the terms that credit card companies use. One is the billing cycle. This is the number of days between statements. Most billing cycles are about thirty days, and you get your bill around the same time each month.

If you don't carry a balance—that is, if you pay your bill in full each month—you have a grace period. This is the time without interest between the statement date and the due date. If you pay all you owe during that period, you pay no interest. Grace periods are usually twenty to thirty days. Some companies don't give a grace period. You definitely want to avoid those companies. If you owe a balance from a previous billing cycle, you don't get a grace period. The minute you make a purchase, interest is charged.

Since statements are mailed or emailed, you might not receive your bill until a few days into the grace period. And the payment needs to be mailed at least several days before the due date to be received on time. So, with a typical twenty-five-day grace period, you might have only fifteen days in which to pay without being charged interest.

Most credit cards have a credit limit. This is the most you can borrow on that card. When you get your first credit card, the limit is likely to be low. As you are smart with credit, paying your bills on time, the limit usually goes up. The important thing is getting that first card.

Myths and Facts

Myth: On a fixed-rate credit card, the rate will never change.

Fact: A company can change the rate on any card if it gives you a notice fifteen days before it goes into effect.

Myth: All you need to pay each month is the minimum payment.

Fact: The less of the bill you pay, the more you pay in interest. Over a period of years, this can mean that you spend thousands of dollars more than you intended to.

Myth: Cards that give cash back or other "freebies" pay for themselves.

Fact: Maybe. "Rewards" cards usually have higher annual fees and higher interest rates. However, if you are disciplined and have the means to pay off your balance every month, you may be able to benefit from the rewards.

Myth: A card's interest rate and annual fee are non-negotiable.

Fact: Not true. Lowering these rates can be as easy as calling your credit card's customer service department. CreditCards.com reports that 69 percent of cardholders who requested a lower interest rate and 82 percent of those who requested lower annual fees succeeded.

CHAPTER THREE

Taking the Plunge into Credit

n order to get a lender to issue you a credit card, they need to decide that you are a good risk. Lenders want to be sure that you will pay what you owe and pay it on time. When you have good credit (credit worthiness), lenders trust you more.

You have to show lenders that you are stable. That means you are at least eighteen years old and have a job. It does not have to be a great job; it just has to produce steady income. The longer you work at the same job, the more credit worthy you are. If you go from job to job, lenders worry that you may be out of work when their bill is due.

Lenders are also skeptical if you move around a lot. Staying in one place for more than six months or a year tells them that you are dependable.

Start with Bank Accounts

Even having a job you don't plan on staying at forever proves to the bank that you are a good credit risk.

You can show lenders that you are dependable with money by opening a bank account. A bank account also gives you a supply of cash that you will need as you learn to handle a credit card. You don't need to have a credit history to open a bank account. After you open the account, you will get a debit card from the bank. Using the card will give you experience purchasing without cash.

Paying bills on time convinces lenders that you are credit worthy. If you have an apartment and pay for electricity or gas, phone, or water, you can use those receipts to prove that you are a good credit risk. If you live at home and pay your parents for your cell phone, cable, or other monthly expense, try to put those bills in your name and pay them directly. That will help establish that you can be trusted with financial responsibilities.

Putting in an Application

When you have demonstrated your stability and ability to manage money, you are ready to apply for a credit card. The best place to start is your bank. If you have an account there and are a good customer, the bank will want to keep your business, even though your account may be small.

Before you apply, however, you have a little homework to do. You should find out the bank's rules for giving out cards. Do you need a minimum deposit of a certain amount? Do you need to be a certain age? If you don't meet the bank's requirements, there is no use filling out an application. In fact, applying for a card that you will not get could actually hurt your chances of getting a different card.

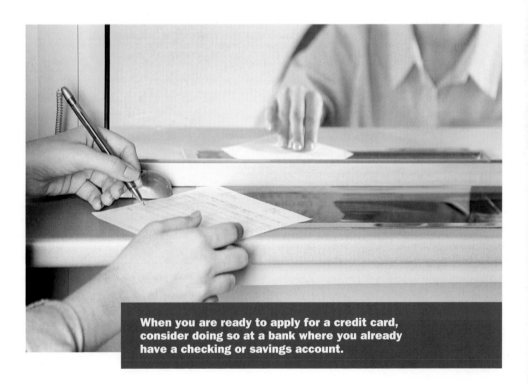

When you are ready to apply for a credit card, consider doing so at a bank where you already have a checking or savings account.

If you meet the basic requirements for applying, you need to find out one other piece of information before you turn in your application: Does the bank report this account to a credit bureau? Credit bureaus keep track of your borrowing activity, and a good track record builds your credit worthiness. Lenders usually report their accounts to the credit bureaus, but they don't have to. If the bank does not report, you should look for a different card. Your goal is not just to obtain a credit card but also to build up a good credit history.

If your bank turns you down, your next choice might be a department store card. Store cards are generally easier to get. For people with no credit history, store cards have low credit limits and high interest rates, but that shouldn't bother you. The point is to establish credit, to get started. So, you don't want to charge very much, and you want to pay what you owe each month. After you have used the card for a while, you will qualify for another card with better terms. At that point, you can cancel the store card. Just be sure that you meet the store's requirements before applying. And find out if the store reports to a credit bureau.

Secured Cards

If you cannot find a bank or store that is willing to give you a credit card, you have one other option. You can get a secured card from a bank. To get a secured card, you have to start with a little cash. You deposit a certain amount of money in the secured account. That money becomes the collateral that secures your loans. It is also your credit limit; you can't borrow any more than the amount of money you deposited. A secured card is safe for the bank. If you don't pay, the bank can always get its money back from your account.

The way to use a secured card to establish credit worthiness is to use it for small purchases and pay the bill as soon as you get it. After a time, the bank will be willing to change it from a secured

People who are unable to prove their credit worthiness to a credit card issuer may want to get a cosigner who agrees to pay the balance in case the main applicant doesn't.

card to an unsecured card. It usually takes about a year for you to prove to the bank that you are ready for an unsecured card.

Getting a Cosigner

One other way to get that all-important first break in establishing credit is with a cosigner. You could apply for a specific loan, say, for a car. Then, you have someone with a good credit history sign the loan agreement along with you. That person, the cosigner, promises to pay the loan back if you don't. When someone cosigns for you, you need to be extra careful to make the payments on time. How you handle the responsibility will affect the credit reputation of both you and the cosigner.

GET YOUR *CREDIT CARD* RIGHT NOW!

BANK NAME

1234 5678 9012 3456

MONTH/YEAR
03/23
CARD HOLDER NAME

☑ No Annual Fee

☑ Earn Cash Back

☑ Low Introductory APR Offer*

APPLY NOW

* Lorem ipsum dolor sit amet, consectetur adipiscing elit, sed do eiusmod tempor incididunt ut labore et dolore magna aliqua. Ut enim ad minim veniam, quis nostrud exercitation ullamco laboris.

Credit cards that do not charge an annual fee or that have other benefits, like low interest rates, are ideal.

The Right Card for You

When you think you've shown that you are credit worthy, how do you decide what is the best card to get? There are so many choices and so much fine print! A good place to start your search is the internet. Just type "choose credit cards" into any search engine and sites will pop up that let you compare cards. You have to select the type of card, or category. First try "no annual fee cards." Cards in the "low interest rate" category are also good. If you are credit smart, you will be paying in full each month and will not need to worry about interest. But problems do happen, so it is a good idea to make sure that your interest rate is as low as you can get.

It may be hard to get a card with every feature you want, so look at the most important feature: APR. Even though companies calculate APR differently, most are very similar. Comparing APRs is still the easiest way to see which card is best. Make sure that the card has a grace period. In selecting and using the card, look out for some of the traps and trip-ups that can cost you money.

10 Great Questions to Ask a Financial Adviser

1. What is the APR?

2. Is this an introductory rate? If so, how long does it last? What is the rate after the introductory rate expires?

3. Is there a fee to apply for the card? If so, how much?

4. Is there an annual fee? If so, how much?

5. What other fees are charged? Late fees? Over-the-limit fees? Others?

6. Is the APR fixed or variable? If it is variable, how does that work?

7. What is the grace period? On what day of the month is my payment due? Can I change this date?

8. How will you tell me of any changes in my contract?

9. Do you report to a credit reporting agency? If so, which one do you use?

10. May I pay my bill online? Are there any fees for using online bill payment?

CHAPTER FOUR

Dangers of Credit Cards

Grocery stores have discovered ways to make more money, such as putting candy bars at the checkouts. Lenders also have techniques that can get you to spend more money than you originally intended to. Be sure to be on the lookout for special fees, promotions, and penalties.

Special Offers

Stores often advertise a popular product at a low price. Sometimes, they will actually lose money selling the product. But they end up making money because people come into their store and buy other items. The same tactic works with credit cards.

Some advertisements for credit cards promise a discount on merchandise when you sign up. Others will give you cash back on your purchases, airline miles, or other goodies. The purpose of these advertisements is to get you to take and use the credit card. A company doesn't mind losing $25 giving you a gift if you will spend $50 with the credit card. The trap is that many cards that offer "freebies" charge higher interest rates and higher fees. You might get 2 percent cash back on your purchases but pay more than that for the benefit. Read the fine print.

Promotional Rates

Have you ever gone into a store for an item you

Credit card companies offer all kinds of items to get people to apply for their cards. In the long run, they know they will make money off of cardholders.

saw advertised and found it wasn't quite what you thought it was? Once you were in the store, you might very well have bought something else. Advertisers call this "bait and switch"—advertise a good deal (the bait) and switch to something else when the customer "bites."

In the selling of credit cards, the bait is an offer of "no annual fee, 0 percent interest for up to a year," or some other teaser. Generally, the company is true to its promise, and you may enjoy no interest or a low rate for a while. But once the introductory period is over, the company often switches to a very high APR. Sometimes, the introductory period is as short as three months. Again, read the fine print.

Know what the numbers mean before you sign. The same APR can result in different amounts of interest, depending on the method of calculation.

When you read the fine print, you will see more than one APR. Banks can have one APR for purchases, another one for balance transfers, and a different one for cash advances. Some banks have tiered APRs, which are different rates for different balances. With a tiered APR, you could pay 15 percent on balances under $500, for example, and 18 percent on balances above that amount. Your normal APR may switch to a penalty APR if you are late on your payment. It's all in the fine print.

Lots of Fees

Another way stores increase their sales is by tacking on extra features—and charging you for them. You might buy a digital camera that is no good unless you buy batteries, too. If you want a carrying case, that is extra. And the memory card is sold separately. With credit cards, the extras are fees. Lenders charge all kinds of fees, including the following:

If you are even one day late with your credit card payment, you can expect to be charged a late fee.

- Account fee, for just having the account. This might be called the annual fee, monthly service fee, or minimum finance fee.
- Late fee, charged when your payment is late (in addition to interest).
- Over-the-limit fee, charged when you borrow more than the limit that is set in your cardholder agreement.
- Transfer fee, for transferring the balance from one account to another.
- Cash advance fee, for borrowing cash.
- Check access fee, for using checks the company sends you in the mail.
- Currency exchange surcharge, for purchasing something from another country (sometimes done over the internet).
- Service fee, for redeeming your rewards (cash back, frequent flyer miles, etc.).

Every creditor does not charge all of these fees. How do you know if yours does? Read the fine print.

An Example of a Bad Credit Decision

What You Do	What You Owe
Get a card with no fee, introductory rate of 1 percent	$ 0.00
Purchase items totaling $1,000	$1,000.00
Pay only the minimum balance of $20	$ 980.00
Interest of $9.80 is added (new balance)	$ 989.80
Pay only the minimum balance of $20	$ 969.80
Interest of $9.70 is added (new balance)	$ 979.50
Pay the minimum balance of $20 late	$ 959.50
Interest of $9.60 is added	$ 969.10
Late fee of $35 is added (new balance)	$1,004.10
Introductory rate expired or cancelled because of late payment, 20 percent Interest of $200.82 is added (new balance)	$1,204.92
Pay the new minimum of $25	$1,179.92
Interest of $235.98 is added (new balance)	$1,415.90

In just five months, you'll owe more than a third more than the items were worth!

Protecting Your Card

When you buy a large appliance, it comes with a warranty. Although you have this guarantee, the salesperson will usually try to sell you an extended warranty. This may or may not be needed. With a credit card, it is totally unnecessary.

Some companies try to sell what they call credit card loss protection. Like a warranty, it is insurance in case you lose your card and someone else tries to use it. If someone racks up a big bill on your card, the company you bought the protection from will pay

If your credit card is lost or stolen, be sure to notify the issuer immediately to prevent fraud.

the bill. The reason you don't need this is that if you report a lost or stolen card, the credit card company will not charge you for most of the purchases that you did not make. By law, the company cannot charge you more than $50 if your card is misused. So, the most you can lose is $50, and credit card loss protection often costs more than that.

Extra Billing

A few credit card companies make a little extra money with two-cycle billing. It's a complicated way of figuring out how much interest you owe. Two-cycle billing follows the average daily balance method but uses figures from two cycles instead of one to calculate that balance. If you carry a balance some months and don't have a balance other months, this billing method can raise your overall interest. The Discover card uses two-cycle billing. The fine print will tell you if a card uses this method.

Making the Minimum Payment

If you read the fine print, you can avoid most credit card traps. You also need to be careful about your own actions that can trip you up. Probably the biggest mistake is making only the minimum payment. Your statement has two numbers telling you what you owe. One is the balance—the total amount you owe. The other is the minimum payment due. The minimum payment is what you have to pay to keep your account. It is usually only 2 to 3 percent of what you actually owe. If you pay only this amount, you will have a balance and will be charged interest on that balance. Every month that you don't pay off the entire balance, more interest is charged. Before long, you can be paying interest on the interest! The smartest way to go is to pay the

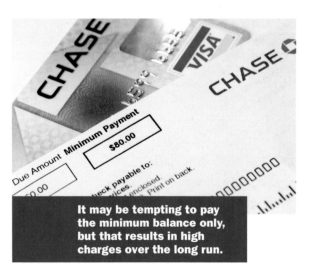

It may be tempting to pay the minimum balance only, but that results in high charges over the long run.

balance in full every time you get your statement and never have to pay interest.

Transferring Balances

Another thing that can trip you up is transferring balances. This is rolling the balance on a high-interest account over into a new account with a lower APR. It might be a good idea if you can find a card with an introductory rate of 0 percent interest that doesn't charge an annual fee. But what if you don't pay the balance off before the introductory rate expires? At this point, you could look for a new account. But rolling your debt over to one new account after another negatively affects your credit score. And that could keep you from qualifying for a low-interest card.

The low introductory rate can be misleading. Sometimes, the promotional rate applies only to the transferred amount. If you use the card for new purchases, interest on the new amount may be charged at the higher, regular rate for the card.

Cash advances on credit cards can be good in an emergency, but they usually involve high fees.

Beware of fees on the new account. The new card may not have an account fee, but it may charge a fee to make the balance transfer. Watch the credit limit. When you transfer debt to a new card, that amount is part of your credit limit. If you start charging on the new card, the old debt plus the new debt could put you over the limit. Remember the over-the-limit fees? They can be high.

If you do have a low-interest balance transfer, you cannot afford to be late on a payment. If you make a late payment on some cards, your interest rate can go from 0 percent to more than 25 percent!

Taking Out a Cash Advance

Don't be tripped up by using credit to get cash. Some banks offer cash advances on your credit card. Even if the APR on your card is low, the fees and interest on cash advances are usually very, very high. If your bank sends you checks for your credit card account, they are not like checks on a checking account. When you write and sign a cash-advance check, you are borrowing money from your bank. You will pay a transaction fee for each check you write, usually $10 at least, plus a much higher interest rate than you pay for other items on your card. And you will pay interest, even if you pay the advance back when you are billed, because cash advances have no grace periods.

Avoiding all of the credit traps and mistakes will help you keep more of your money. It will also help you develop something really important to being able to borrow in the future: a great credit score.

CHAPTER FIVE

Credit Scores and Why They Matter

n order for lenders to know whether you are likely to repay what you have borrowed, they check your credit report. The report tells the reporting agency, or credit bureau, information about what loans and credit cards you have with a number of stores and banks.

Seven-Year Report

A credit report shows how you have handled credit for at least the past seven years. Every time you apply for or use credit, information goes into the report. The report contains four sections:

- Personal information. Along with the basics, the report has your Social Security number and a list of places where you have worked.

- Account information. The report lists your credit accounts, their limits, and how many payments were on time or late thirty days, sixty days, or ninety days.
- Public information. Any government action that affects your finances appears on your report. If a company sued you because you did not pay your bills, that action will be listed.
- Inquiries. Any company that asks to see your credit report shows up on the report. The report also tells why the inquiry, or request, was made.

Why Your Credit Report Matters

A number of different people can get a copy of your credit report. When you apply for a loan or a credit card, you authorize the lender to see your report. Any time you apply, even if you don't get the loan, new information is added to your report. People looking at the report will know all of the times you have applied for credit and where.

If you have credit accounts with a bank or company, those companies

A good credit score assures banks that you are a good risk. A high score can net you a low interest rate.

often want to keep tabs on your credit activity. They might want to raise or lower your credit limit or change your APR. So they access your report to monitor your account.

Any company that is doing significant business with you can look at your report. Even people who are not lending you money, such as landlords and insurance companies, want to be sure that you are the kind of person who pays your bills on time. Sometimes, when you apply for a job, an employer will ask permission to access your credit report.

Getting a Free Credit Report

You can get a copy of your credit report. In fact, you can get three copies every year for free. And you should. Credit reports do more

Large credit reporting agencies are also vulnerable to data breaches. A breach in September 2017 exposed the sensitive information of almost 150 million customers.

than protect companies against lending money to people who are bad risks. They protect you, too. They let you know who is asking about you. If anyone has stolen any of your financial information and is trying to use it, that will show up on the report, too. (See chapter 6.)

Businesses report your information to one of three bureaus: Experian, Equifax, and TransUnion. These agencies may not all have the same information, so the reports may be slightly different. The three worked together to create a central place from which you can access your report. The Fair and Accurate Credit Transaction Act, passed by Congress in 2003, gives you the right to a free credit report from each agency once a year. You can get a combined report or separate reports from each agency. It's a good idea to get a report from one of the agencies one month, a report from a second agency three or four months later, and a report from the last agency three or four months after that.

You can get your report by phone or by going online at https://www.annualcreditreport.com. If you want to access the reports online, make sure you are going to the https://www.annualcreditreport.com

Be sure to promptly dispute any mistakes you find on your credit report.

site. If you go to each agency's website, you can obtain a report, but it will not be free.

You might see advertisements from other companies that offer free credit reports. These companies, like banks, are in business to make money. So why would they offer you something for free? Because they want to sell you something else. When you receive a free report from these companies, you usually have signed up for credit monitoring. The company will monitor, or keep watch on, your credit and let you know of any suspicious activity—for a monthly fee. You can monitor your accounts yourself for free.

Raising Your Credit Score

The following are some steps you can take to raise your credit score:

- Pay all of your bills on time.
- If you miss a payment, pay it as soon as possible.
- If you have to carry a balance on a credit card for a time, keep it as low as possible.
- Pay off revolving credit rather than transferring it to a new account.
- Don't open new credit accounts unless you really need them.
- Check your credit report regularly and correct any errors.

You might find mistakes on your credit report. The information is supplied and recorded by people, and people make mistakes. The report will explain how to correct anything that is wrong. Make the corrections right away. Your credit report is a snapshot of you, and you want the picture to be accurate. Besides, the information affects another important number: your credit score.

What Makes Up Your Credit Score?

Your credit score is a number that lenders use to rate how risky it is to lend money to you. The higher the number, the better risk you are. Your credit score is not the only factor in their decision, but it is a big one. The number is calculated from information

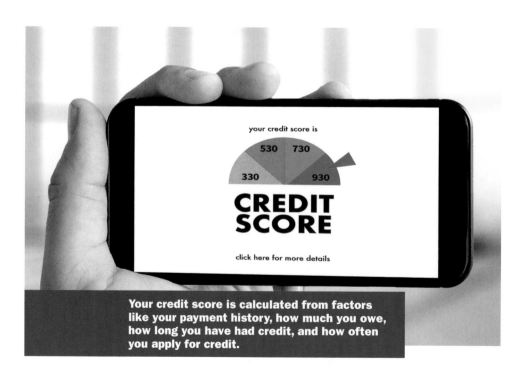

Your credit score is calculated from factors like your payment history, how much you owe, how long you have had credit, and how often you apply for credit.

in your credit reports. The number most lenders use is called the FICO score.

The FICO score considers five factors, and some are more important than others. Just as a grade in a class at school might be 50 percent dependent on test scores, 30 percent on homework assignments, and 20 percent on class participation, each of the factors in the FICO score has a certain weight. The factors are as follows:

- **Payment history (35 percent)**. Whether or not you pay on time is obviously the most important indicator of how good a credit risk you are.
- **Amount owed (30 percent)**. This factor compares the total amount you owe with the total amount you can borrow (credit limit). A number of 20 percent or under is good.
- **Length of credit history (15 percent)**. The longer you have had good credit, the better your score will be. This factor is only 15 percent of your total score, so even if you have little or no credit history, you can still have a good score.
- **New credit (10 percent)**. This factor measures new accounts that you have opened and inquiries into your credit report. If you have a lot of inquiries because you are trying to open several new accounts, you don't look like a good credit risk. But if you are trying to buy a car, for example, you might have a number of inquiries all around the same time because you are looking for the best deal for financing. These are all treated as one inquiry. When you ask for a copy of your credit report, this is not counted as an inquiry and does not lower your score.

- **Types of credit (10 percent)**. Lenders like to see a variety of credit in your history. Credit cards are for short-term loans. Installment loans, such as auto loans, are for longer terms. If some of your credit is in long-term loans, you look more stable.

FICO scores range from 300 to 850. Lenders consider scores above 750 excellent and scores below 600 poor. If you want to know your credit score, you can get it from one of the credit bureaus that issues credit reports. The reports are free, but you have to pay for the credit score.

If your score is lower than you want or your credit report is not very healthy, you can change it. It will take time and discipline, but you can do it. Your credit history will follow you for the rest of your life. It's worth getting under control. And it's worth guarding.

CHAPTER SIX

Protecting Your Credit

After you have done all the planning and effort to establish credit, you need to make sure you protect your cards and card numbers from being stolen. A related problem to watch out for is identity theft.

The US Federal Trade Commission (FTC) estimates that around three million Americans have their identities stolen each year, resulting in losses of nearly a billion dollars in 2017. Identity thieves get hold of some information about you and use that information to rent an apartment, open a credit card account, buy a car, or run up health care costs. You may not even know that your identity has been stolen until a bill collector comes to call or you review your credit report.

Keep Your Personal Info Secret

You are probably very careful to keep your cash and credit cards from being stolen. You need to be just as careful with your

Unless you are careful, thieves looking for personal information may find it in your trash.

personal information. Guard all of your numbers: Social Security, birth date, address, phone, and bank accounts. A clever thief can use any of these numbers.

Your Social Security number is your primary identification. Don't carry it with you. Memorize it and keep it in a safe place. Your employer and your bank are probably the only ones that need to know your number. If some other businesses ask for it, find out why they need it.

You should be able to do business without giving out this very private information.

You don't want any other number to fall into the hands of thieves, either. Thieves go through the trash to find numbers they can use. So before you throw away receipts, letters, or other

Be careful when entering your PIN into an ATM in a public place. You never know who is watching.

papers, shred them. You should even shred offers that you receive for credit cards.

Thieves also look through mailboxes. If you're paying bills by mail and thieves steal those payments, they have your name, address, bank account number, and maybe even credit card information. Take your mail to a box at the post office. The mail that comes to your house has valuable information on it also. To be really safe, you should either have a locked mailbox or use a box at the post office.

Guard your personal identification numbers (PINs) like you would your Social Security number. Choose PINs and passwords that are hard for other people to guess but easy for you to remember. Don't write them down and leave them where others can see them.

Check that the "s" appears at the end of the https:// of a website's address to make sure it has some level of security.

If you receive a phone call or an email asking you to verify any of your identifying information, don't do it! The people who need that information already have it. Identity thieves can be very clever, especially the ones who stalk the internet. They can cut and paste bank logos so that their emails look like they are coming from your bank. Banks never send their customers emails requesting information. Be very careful about links that you click on from emails because they could take you to fake websites that are trying to get your personal information.

As you do more and more business over the internet, it's very important that you have a secure browser—the kind that scrambles the financial information you send electronically. Check with your internet provider to make sure. When you purchase items over the internet, use your credit card instead of your debit card.

How Identity Thieves Work

- **Dumpster diving.** They rummage through the trash looking for items with your personal information on it.

- **Skimming.** They steal card numbers by using a special storage device when processing your card. Skimmers can be placed on gas pumps and ATMs, for example.

- **Phishing.** They pretend to be financial institutions or companies and send spam or pop-up messages to get you to reveal your personal information.

- **Changing your address.** They divert your billing statements to another location by completing a change-of-address form.

- **Old-fashioned stealing.** They steal wallets and purses; mail, including bank and credit card statements; preapproved credit offers; and new checks or tax information. They steal personnel records or bribe employees who have access.

- **Pretexting.** They use false pretenses to obtain your personal information from financial institutions, telephone companies, and other sources.

Learn more at IdentityTheft.gov.

With a debit card, your money is gone right away. With a credit card, the creditor will help you resolve problems that might come up.

What to Do If It Happens to You

Identity thieves steal more than your identity. They steal your name as a trustworthy borrower. As soon as you're aware that someone has done this to you, you need to take steps to get your good name back. The first step is to stop the thieves from stealing more than they already have. The way to stop them is to place a fraud alert on your credit report.

A fraud alert is a statement that your information has been stolen. When the thief tries to open any new credit in your name, he or she has to fill out a credit application. Remember what the lender does with that application? The lender requests a credit report. The lender will see on the report that someone has used your information without your permission. The lender will contact you to see if you or the thief filled out the application.

To file a fraud alert, contact one of the three credit reporting agencies. Any one of them will contact the other two and see that the alert is on all of them.

Identity theft can be a nightmare of bill collectors, cancelled accounts, denied applications, and a ruined reputation. It is more than a hassle; it is a serious crime. To fix all of the problems it causes, you need to file two forms: a police Identity Theft Report and an ID Theft Complaint. You can find details on how to obtain these documents on the FTC website, IdentityTheft.gov.

Once you have these documents, you can dispute, or disagree with, charges to your account. From your credit report, find out which charges are yours and which were made by the thief. Then, send letters or online forms to the three credit reporting agencies,

Identity theft can result in serious jail time for offenders.

disputing the charges that are not yours. You have to contact each agency. Enclose copies of the two reports. Make sure you keep a copy of the letter. You also need to send dispute letters to all of the lenders that think you owe them money. Mail them by certified mail, and include copies of the Identity Theft Report and ID Theft Complaint.

When identity theft happens to you, it takes a lot of work to fix it. But you can do it. Repairing the damage is worth whatever time and energy it takes. In today's world, it is nearly impossible to do business without credit. If you understand how credit works, read the fine print on your credit applications and statements, avoid the common traps and mistakes, monitor your credit reports, and guard your personal information, you'll have what it takes to live smart in today's credit card world.

GLOSSARY

adjusted balance The method of calculating interest in which the interest is figured and the balance adjusted once in a billing cycle.

annual percentage rate (APR) The interest rate charged on a credit card balance in a one-year period. The actual interest charged each month is the APR divided by twelve.

ATM card A card that is used at an automated teller machine (ATM) to make deposits or withdrawals to a bank account.

average daily balance A method of calculating interest on the average of each day's balances in a billing cycle.

balance The amount of money that is owed on an account.

billing cycle The number of days between credit card statements.

collateral Property used to secure a loan. The property can be taken by the creditor if the loan is not repaid.

credit bureau An agency that keeps a history of people's borrowing activity on file and reports that information to creditors.

credit limit The highest amount you are allowed to borrow on a card.

creditor The person or institution that lends money; a lender.

credit worthiness The quality of having a good credit history and, therefore, being a good credit risk.

debit card A card issued by a bank that looks like a credit card but is actually used like a check. When it is used, money is debited, or subtracted, from the account.

FICO score The measure of credit worthiness developed by and named for the Fair Isaac Corporation.

grace period The interest-free time between the credit card statement date and the due date. If a bill is paid in full before the grace period ends, no interest is charged.

installment loan A loan that is paid back in equal payments over a set period of time.

interest A fee for using money. A bank pays interest to depositors, and a lender charges interest on the money it lends out.

lender A person or institution that lends money; a creditor.

revolving account A credit card account that is billed and paid once a month.

secured credit Loans that are safe for the lender because they are backed up by something worth at least as much as the amount of the loan.

tiered APR The charging of different interest rates depending on the balance on the account.

unsecured credit Loans that are not backed up by anything that can guarantee repayment.

variable rate An interest rate that varies, or changes, according to changes in some other figure to which it is connected.

FOR MORE INFORMATION

Annual Credit Report Request Service
PO Box 105283
Atlanta, GA 30348-5283
Website: https://www.annualcreditreport.com
This service's website provides free copies of
    credit reports.

Equifax
PO Box 740241
Atlanta, GA 30374-0241
(866) 349-5191
Website: http://www.equifax.com
Facebook: @Equifax
Twitter: @EquifaxInsights
This credit reporting agency provides credit management
    information to businesses and individual consumers.

Equifax Canada, Inc.
7100 Jean-Talon Street, Suite 1000
Montreal, QC H1M 0A3
(800) 465-7166
Website: http://www.equifax.com/EFX_Canada
Twitter: @equifaxcanada
Equifax Canada is a credit reporting agency that provides
    credit management information to businesses and
    individual consumers.

Experian
475 Anton Boulevard
Costa Mesa, CA 92626
(888) 397-3742
Website: http://www.experian.com
Facebook and Instagram: @Experian
Twitter: @Experian_US
Experian is a credit reporting agency that provides
     credit management information to businesses and
     individual consumers.

Fair Isaac Corporation
181 Metro Drive
San Jose, CA 95110 USA
(408) 817-9100
Website: http://www.myfico.com
Facebook and Twitter: @myfico
Fair Isaac Corporation developed scores of credit
     worthiness and provides explanations and helpful
     information about credit.

Federal Trade Commission (FTC)
600 Pennsylvania Avenue NW
Washington, DC 20580
(202) 326-2222
Website: http://www.ftc.gov
Facebook: @federaltradecommission
Twitter: @FTC
The FTC is a national government agency that
     protects consumers from unfair or dishonest
     business practices.

Financial Planning Standards Council (FPSC)
902–375 University Avenue
Toronto, ON M5G 2J5
Canada
(800) 305-9886
Email: inform@fpsc.ca
Website: http://www.fpsc.ca
Facebook: @FPSC.Canada
Twitter: @FPSC_Canada
FPSC provides information for teens on personal finance,
       budgeting, savings, investments, and more.

Jump$tart Coalition for Personal Financial Literacy
1001 Connecticut Avenue NW, Suite 640
Washington, DC 20036
(202) 846-6780
Email: info@jumpstart.org
Website: http://www.jumpstart.org
Facebook and Twitter: @natljumpstart
Jump$tart offers information on credit, money
       management, budgeting, investing, savings,
       and more. Its clearinghouse lists helpful books
       and websites.

FOR FURTHER READING

Bickerstaff, Linda. *Smart Strategies for Saving and Building Wealth.* New York, NY: Rosen Publishing, 2015.

Blohm, Craig E. *Teen Guide to Credit and Debt.* San Diego, CA: ReferencePoint Press, Inc., 2017.

Hardyman, Robyn. *Understanding Credit and Debt.* New York, NY: Rosen Publishing, 2018.

Marsico, Katie. *Using Credit Wisely.* Ann Arbor, MI: Cherry Lake Publishing, 2016.

McGuire, Kara. *Making Money Work: The Teens' Guide To Saving, Investing, and Building Wealth.* North Mankato, MN: Capstone Young Readers, 2015.

McGuire, Kara. *The Teen Money Manual: A Guide to Cash, Credit, Spending, Saving, Work, Wealth, and More.* North Mankato, MN: Capstone Young Readers, 2015.

Minden, Cecelia. *Living on a Budget.* Ann Arbor, MI: Cherry Lake Publishing, 2016.

Nagle, Jeanne. *Money, Banking, and Finance.* New York, NY: Rosen Publishing, 2018.

Schlesinger, Emily, and Jennifer Liss. *Managing Money.* Costa Mesa, CA: Saddleback Educational Publishing, 2017.

Weeks, Marcus, and Derek Braddon. *Heads Up Money.* New York, NY: DK Publishing, 2016.

BIBLIOGRAPHY

ByDesign Financial Solutions. *Financial Firsts: Your Guide to a Solid Financial Future.* Los Angeles, CA: ByDesign, 2006.

Fair Isaac Corporation. *Your Credit Score.* Retrieved October 19, 2018. http://www.myfico.com /Downloads/Files/myFICO_YCS_Booklet.pdf.

Federal Trade Commission. "Credit Education Center." Retrieved October 19, 2018. http://www.myfico .com/CreditEducation.

Federal Trade Commission. "FTC Releases Annual Summary of Complaints Reported by Consumers." March 6, 2018. http://www.ftc.gov/news-events /press-releases/2018/03/ftc-releases-annual -summary-complaints-reported-consumers.

Fowles, Debby. *7 Common Credit Card Myths.* The Motley Fool. https://www.fool.com/credit -cards/2017/09/30/7-common-credit-card-myths .aspx

Frankel, Matthew. *1,000 Best Smart Money Secrets for Students.* Naperville, IL: Sourcebooks, 2005.

Pahl, Greg. *The Unofficial Guide to Beating Debt.* Chicago, IL: IDG Books, 2000.

INDEX

A

annual fee, 22, 28, 31, 33
annual percentage rate
   (APR), 18–19, 20, 28,
   32
ATM cards, 14–15

B

balance transfer, 33, 37–38
bank accounts, 10, 24
billing, two-cycle, 36
billing cycle, 21
bill payment, 24, 27, 32,
   36, 38, 45

C

cardholder agreement, 16,
   18, 33
cash advance, 33, 38
collateral, 11, 26
cosigner, 27
credit
  from banks, 7–10
  secured, 11, 26
  from stores, 10–11
  types of, 11
  unsecured, 11, 12, 27
credit card(s)
  age requirements, 23, 25

agreement, 16, 18, 33
application, 25–26, 27,
   39, 40
balance, 21, 36–37, 43
benefits of, 13
choosing, 28
dangers of, 13, 30–33,
   35–38
fees, 32–33
myths and facts, 22
rewards, 22, 33
statements, 15, 18, 21,
   36–37, 51
credit history, 13, 24, 26,
   27, 45, 46
credit limit, 21, 26, 38, 45
creditors and lenders, 7,
   15, 23, 30, 52
credit report, 38, 39–46
credit score, 43, 44–46
credit worthiness, 23, 26,
   28, 44, 45

D

debit card, 14–15, 24, 52
Discover card, 36
disputed charges, 52, 54

E
employment, 23, 41
F
Fair and Accurate Credit
    Transaction Act, 42
Federal Deposit Insurance
    Company (FDIC), 10
fees, 32–33
FICO score, 44, 45, 46
financial advisor, questions
    for, 29
financial institutions, 7, 8,
    11, 12, 51
fine print, 16, 21, 31, 33,
    36, 54
fixed interest rates, 20–
    21, 22
G
grace period, 21, 28, 38
I
identity theft, 47, 51, 52, 54
installment loans, 17, 45
interest, 8, 15, 20, 36–37
  on credit cards, 11, 13, 18,
      20–21, 22, 37, 38
  example calculations of,
      8–9, 18–20, 34
  rates, 18, 20, 22, 26, 28,
      31, 38
  0 percent, 31, 37, 38
L
loss protection, 35

M
Mastercard, 12
minimum payment, 5, 22, 36
P
penalties, 32
promotional offers, 31, 37
R
revolving account, 17–18,
    43
S
secured card, 26–27
seven-year report, 39–40
special offers, 31–32
store credit cards, 10–11,
    26–27
V
variable interest rate, 20
Visa, 12–13

ABOUT THE AUTHORS

Xina M. Uhl has authored a variety of books for young people in addition to textbooks, teacher's guides, lessons, and assessment questions. When she is not writing or reading, she enjoys travel, photography, and hiking with her dogs. Her blog features her travel adventures and latest fiction projects.

Ann Byers works in a youth organization as director of programs for teen parents. One of the goals of her work is to help young people move toward independence. She helps them transition successfully into jobs, housing, and financial health. That includes showing them how to be credit smart.

PHOTO CREDITS

Cover PeopleImages/E+/Getty Images; cover, p. 1 (wallet logo) logomills/Shutterstock.com; p. 5 wavebreakmedia/Shutterstock.com; p. 8 Arnaldo Jr/Shutterstock.com; p. 9 © AP Photo; p. 10 Dragon Images/Shutterstock.com; p. 12 Cassiohabib/Shutterstock.com; p. 14 Olga Kashubin/Shutterstock.com; p. 17 jason cox/Shutterstock.com; p. 18 Smith Collection/Gado/Archive Photos/Getty Images; p. 20 Georgejmclittle/Shutterstock.com; p. 24 Nomad Soul/Shutterstock.com; p. 25 Africa Studio/Shutterstock.com; p. 27 Eric Audras/ONOKY/Getty Images; p. 28 AleksOrel/Shutterstock.com; p. 31 Jeff Greenberg/Universal Images Group/Getty Images; p. 32 Kreative Photography/Alamy Stock Photo; p. 33 gemphoto/Shutterstock.com; p. 35 ALPA PROD/Shutterstock.com; p. 36 Alpha and Omega Collection/Alamy Stock Photo; p. 37 Andrey Arkusha/Shutterstock.com; p. 40 Casper1774 Studio/Shutterstock.com; p. 41 Piotr Swat/Shutterstock.com; p. 42 James R. Martin/Shutterstock.com; p. 44 one photo/Shutterstock.com; p. 48 Peter Dazeley/Photographer's Choice/Getty Images; p. 49 Bukowski Ilya/Shutterstock.com; p. 50 Marc Bruxelle/Shutterstock.com; p. 53 Zoka74/Shutterstock.com.

Design: Raúl Rodriguez, R studio T, NYC;
Layout: Tahara Anderson; Photo Researcher: Sherri Jackson